CELEBRATING
Christmas

CELEBRATING
Christmas

EDITED BY
Glorya Hale
and Carol Kelly-Gangi

2002 **Metro**Books

ISBN 1-58663-584-0

Book design by Rhea Braunstein
Illustrations by Alli Arnold

Printed and bound in the United States of America

02 03 04 05 06 MC 9 8 7 6 5 4 3 2 1

KP

Contents

Introduction

If you had to sum up Christmas in a line or two, what would you say? Charles Schulz simply called it a together time. Leigh Hunt deemed it the glorious time of great Too-Much. Edna Ferber said it isn't a season, but a feeling. So many people, so many voices—all chiming in on the wonders of Christmas.

Celebrating Christmas creates a lively chorus from these diverse voices. Some contributors offer cherished memories of holiday rituals: Russell Baker vividly describes his family's annual quest for the perfect tree; Truman Capote and Dorothy Thompson describe the makeshift decorations they lovingly crafted for the holidays. Others speak of Christmases far from home and loved ones, when the holidays take on a meaning apart from all the trimmings: In the midst of war, General Robert E. Lee pens a thoughtful letter to his wife on Christmas, 1861; Louisa May Alcott shares experiences of a Christmas unlike any she described in *Little Women*.

When all the packages have been ripped open (and you're frantically searching for receipts), take a break with the "Christmas Wrap-Up" section, which gathers reflections on the holiday season just past and musings on the future: Robert Lynd captures the feeling of hope that naturally accompanies the beginning of a new year; Alfred, Lord Tennyson repeats his stirring exhortation to ring out the old and ring in the new.

If you ask 100 people what Christmas means to them, you'll get as many answers. But maybe we can all agree with Christopher Morley who wrote: "Just for a few hours on Christmas Eve and Christmas Day, the stupid, harsh mechanism of the world runs down, and we permit ourselves to live according to untrammeled common sense, the unconquerable efficiency of good will."

CAROL KELLY-GANGI

2002

'Tis the Season

Christmas is a together time.

CHARLES SCHULZ, *American cartoonist*

Yesterday morning at quarter of seven all the children were up and dressed and began to hammer at the door of their mother's and my room, in which their six stockings, all bulging out with queer angles and rotundities, were hanging from the fireplace. So their mother and I got up, shut the window, lit the fire, taking down the stockings, of course, put on our wrappers, and prepared to admit the children.

THEODORE ROOSEVELT, *26th president of the United States*

My favorite Christmas tradition is making Norwegian cookies with my mom. We buy the ingredients together, then make a big mess in the kitchen.

RENEE ZELLWEGER, *American actor*

The greatest gift my father came with, he had funny stories to tell, and happy songs for us to sing while he played his harmonica. There was a moment during all this that an astonishing thought went loping across my mind. I looked at the walls of that little house, at the cedar that sagged to the left, at the Christmas star that had warped, and I thought, "This is a beautiful place."

LEON HALE, *American journalist*

Christmas is a kindling of new fires.

GLADYS TABER, *American archaeologist*

My friend wants our tree to blaze "like a Baptist window," droop with weighty snows of ornament. But we can't afford the made-in-Japan splendors at the five-and-dime. So we do what we've always done: sit for days at the kitchen table with scissors and crayons and stacks of colored paper. I make sketches and my friend cuts them out: lots of cats, fish too (because they're easy to draw), some apples, some watermelons, a few winged angels devised from saved-up sheets of Hershey-bar tin foil. We use safety pins to attach these creations to the tree; as a final touch, we sprinkle the branches with shredded cotton (picked in August for this purpose).

TRUMAN CAPOTE, *American writer*

I had a stocking this year, full of sweets and cigars, and mouth-organs and cherry brandy.

DYLAN THOMAS, *Welsh poet*

They lighted the candles on the Christmas tree, and the young people capered about and were brimming over with secrets and shouted with delight, and the tree shone and glistened brave in its gay trimming of walnuts covered with gold and silver paper, and little bags sewed with bright worsted, and all sorts of pretty homemade trifles. But when the real presents were discovered, the presents that meant no end of thought and management and secret self-denial, the brightest part of the household love and happiness shone out.

SARAH ORNE JEWETT, *American writer*

The children had such a number of gifts that I made a Christmas tree for them; Mother, Aunt, and Liz came down to see it; all said it was something new to them. I never saw one but learned from some of the German stories I had been reading.

MRS. JAMES ROACH, *niece of Jefferson Davis, writing in 1851*

At Christmastime we pile the board
With meat and fruit and vintage stored,
And mid the laughter and the glow
We tread a measure soft and slow,
And kiss beneath the mistletoe.

Author Unknown

Mother accelerated the stocking hanging. Twelve were hung. The foresighted had reserved Big Granny's weeks ahead, the laggards settled for the cook's (first choice) or Mother's (second choice). Each long black stocking hung with a name on it in Mother's bedroom. Five o'clock next morning everybody was scrambling round the fireplace, feeling in the dark for his. So you took down your knobby stocking and in the light of the fire you dug in.

LILLIAN SMITH, *American novelist and civil rights worker*

We had no chimney in our home, but the stocking-hanging was a ceremony nevertheless. My parents, and especially my mother, entered into it with the best of humor. They always put up their own stockings or permitted us to do it for them—and they always laughed next morning when they found potatoes or ears of corn in them. I can now see that my mother's laugh had a tear in it, for she loved pretty things and seldom got any during the years that we lived in the coulee.

HAMLIN GARLAND, *American writer*

My mother weaned me from Christmas stockings by gradually increasing the proportion of oranges and nuts until it became clear that she was no longer interested in accumulating things to fill them.

MARY CATHERINE BATESON,
American anthropologist and writer

My children teased me because their stockings inevitably contained toothbrushes, toothpaste, nail cleaners, soap, washcloths, etc. They said Mother never ceased to remind them that cleanliness was next to godliness—even on Christmas morning.

ELEANOR ROOSEVELT, *American first lady*

On Christmas Eve, and yesterday, there were little branches of mistletoe hanging in several parts of our house, in the kitchen, the entries, the parlor, and the smoking room—suspended from the gas-fittings. The maids of the house did their utmost to entrap the gentleman boarders, old and young, under these privileged places, and there to kiss them, after which they were expected to pay a shilling. It is very queer, being customarily so respectful, that they should assume this license now, absolutely trying to pull the gentlemen into the kitchen by main force, and kissing the harder and more abundantly, the more they were resisted. A little rosy-cheeked Scotch lass—at other times very modest—was the most active in this business. I doubt whether any gentleman but myself escaped.

NATHANIEL HAWTHORNE,
American Consul in Liverpool and novelist

Custom dictates that carolers be asked in and offered a cookie, a piece of cake, something to nibble . . . otherwise the spirit of Christmas will leave your house, and even if you be rich as Midas, your holiday will be sad and mean.

GARRISON KEILLOR, *American humorist*

In staging the school's Christmas play the whole town helped or meddled: older men repaired the platform, assembled the crib; young ones fashioned new innkeepers and freshened the masks with paint. Women made doll babies, and children drew colored pictures of Christmas dinner food, mostly desserts. . . . The church programs were more formal—sermons, choirs, recitations by the children and prizes for the ones who managed to get through them without stuttering, crying, or freezing up—but the school program, featuring the Nativity and involving the whole town, was older, having started before the churches were even built.

From Paradise *by* TONI MORRISON

Our children await Christmas presents like politicians getting election returns: there's the Uncle Fred precinct and the Aunt Ruth district still to come in.

MARCELENE COX, *American writer*

No matter how many Christmas presents you give your child, there's always that terrible moment when he's opened the very last one. That's when he expects you to say, "Oh yes, I almost forgot," and take him out and show him the pony.

MIGNON MCLAUGHLIN, *American writer and humorist*

The only suitable gift for the man who has everything is your deepest sympathy.

IMOGENE FEY, *American writer*

As a kid, sometimes my Christmas present was an orange. We were poor and fruit was a once-a-year thing. To this day that's why I still love the smell of oranges.

DOLLY PARTON, *American singer*

So much, indeed, is there to be said for and against any view about giving presents, that it is safer not to think about it, but to buy your presents first, and afterward to consider what, if anything, you will do with them. After all, if you decide in the end not to give them to anyone, you can always keep them.

ROSE MACAULAY, *English writer*

The first rule in buying Christmas presents is to select something shiny. If the chosen object is of leather, the leather must look as of leather, the leather must look as if it had been well greased; if of silver, it must gleam with the light that never was on sea or land. This is because the wariest person will often mistake shininess for expensiveness.

P. G. WODEHOUSE, *English humorist*

The shepherds came from out the north,
Their coats were brown and old;
They brought Him little newborn lambs—
They had not any gold.

SARA TEASDALE, *American poet*

One should, I think, always give children money, for they will spend it for themselves far more profitably than we can ever spend it for them.

ROSE MACAULAY, *English writer*

One doesn't forget the rounded wonder in the eyes of a boy as he comes bursting upstairs on Christmas morning and finds the two-wheeler or the fire truck of which for weeks he scarcely dared dream.

MAX LERNER, *American educator*

What's your rule for purchasing a present? Mine is: Would I like it? Who knows what anyone else likes, but if I like it, that at least is something.

RUTH GORDON, *American actor*

The magi, as you know, were wise men—wonderfully wise men—who brought gifts to the Babe in the manger. They invented the art of giving Christmas presents. Being wise, their gifts were no doubt wise ones, possibly bearing the privilege of exchange in case of duplication.

From "The Gift of the Magi" by O. HENRY

Christmas is the day when any gift, however small, should be gratefully received provided it is given with love.

CLARE BOOTH LUCE, *American playwright*

Christmas isn't a season.
It's a feeling.

EDNA FERBER,
American novelist and playwright

Once the dollars are removed from Christmas gifts, gift giving becomes more loving, more interesting, and more fun for everyone. Gifts can be found on the seashore, created out of scraps, searched for at book sales, or baked in an oven. Dare to be different. Take the dollars out of gifts and wrap them in love.

D. W. WOODLIFF

"Presents," I often say, "endear Absents."

CHARLES LAMB, *English essayist and humorist*

Not what we give, but what we share,
For the gift without the giver is bare.

JAMES RUSSELL LOWELL, *American poet*

Giving requires good sense.

OVID, *Roman poet*

Do give books—religious or otherwise—for Christmas. They're never fattening, seldom sinful, and permanently personal.

LENORE HERSHEY, *American writer*

Adults can take a simple holiday for children and screw it up. What began as a presentation of simple gifts to delight and surprise children around the Christmas tree has culminated in a woman opening up six shrimp forks from her dog, who drew her name.

ERMA BOMBECK, *American humorist*

The ideal Christmas present is money. The only trouble is, you can't charge it.

BILL VAUGHAN, *American journalist*

The best of all gifts around any Christmas tree: The presence of a happy family all wrapped up in each other.

BURTON HILLIS, *American writer*

Probably the reason we all go so haywire at Christmastime with the endless unrestrained and often silly buying of gifts is that we don't quite know how to put our love into words.

HARLAN MILLER, *American writer*

And on Christmas morning, after the gifts have been opened, what are the kids doing? Playing with boxes and snapping the air pockets of plastic packing material.

ERMA BOMBECK, *American humorist*

When the doorman where I live puts up the Christmas tree in the lobby, he has the same friendly smile for those who have remembered him at Christmas and for those who have not. Except that when he trims the tree, if you have not, there you are on the tree hanging in effigy.

SELMA DIAMOND, *American humorist*

For months they have lain in wait, dim shapes lurking in the forgotten corner of houses and factories all over the country and now they are upon us, sodden with alcohol, their massive bodies bulging with strange green protuberances, attacking us in our homes, at our friends' homes, at our offices—there is no escape, it is the hour of the fruitcake.

DEBORAH PAPIER, *American writer*

Thirty-four years ago I inherited the family fruitcake. Fruitcake is the only food durable enough to become a family heirloom.

RUSSELL BAKER, *American writer*

Ho, Ho, Ho!

Was there ever a wider and more loving conspiracy than that which keeps the venerable figure of Santa Claus from slipping away, with all the other old time myths, into the forsaken wonderland of the past?

HAMILTON WRIGHT MABIE, *American editor and critic*

Christmas is sleeping with one eye shut while the other eye watches for Santa Claus.

CHARLES SCHULZ, *American cartoonist*

They err who thinks Santa Claus comes down the chimney; he really enters through the heart.

MRS. PAUL M. ELL

The great thing is not to believe in Santa Claus; it is to be Santa Claus.

PAT BOONE, *American singer*

The fantasy of Santa Claus serves our children well, in so many ways, that we as parents should join them in wishing him season's greetings.

BRUNO BETTELHEIM, *Austrian-born American psychotherapist*

A cynic is a man who found out when he was about ten that there wasn't any Santa Claus, and he's still upset.

JAMES GOULD COZZENS, *American novelist*

I never believed in Santa Claus because I knew no white man would be coming into my neighborhood after dark.

DICK GREGORY, *American humorist*

What Anarchist started the notion that Santa Claus should dress in red? When I was a boy Santa Claus, whether corporeally present at a Christmas tree or merely ideally described, always wore a fur coat, as is appropriate to his northern home and to the season, and, as stated in Moore's poem, " 'Twas the Night Before Christmas," which I was trained to regard as the standard book authority on Santa Claus. Who is responsible for rigging him out in red?

STEPHEN T. BYINGTON,
in a 1913 letter to the New York Times

Like everyone in his right mind, I feared Santa Claus.

ANNIE DILLARD, *American poet and naturalist*

Dear Santa Claus: I Havent Had Any Christmas Tree in 4 Years And I Have Broken My Trimmings And I want A Pair of Roller Skates And A Book, I Cant Think of Any Thing More. I Want You to Think of Something More. Good By.

EDSEL FORD, *American President of the Ford Motor Company,*
in a letter to Santa Claus written when he was eight years old

As the visits of Santa Claus in the night could only be through the chimney, we hung our stockings where they would be in full sight. We had a genuine fireplace in our kitchen, big enough to contain an enormous back log, and broad enough for eight or ten people to form "a circle wide" before it and enjoy the genial warmth.

The last process before going to bed was to suspend our stocking in the chimney jambs; and then we dreamed of Santa Claus, or if we awoke in the night, we listened for the jingling of his sleigh bells.

THEODORE LEDYARD CUYLER, *American clergyman*

Here comes old Father Christmas,
    With sound of fife and drums;
With mistletoe about his brows,
    So merrily he comes!
His arms are full of all good cheer,
    His face with laughter glows,
He shines like any household fire
    Amid the cruel snows.

ROSE TERRY COOKE, *American poet and writer*

The Christmas Spirit

Dearer than memory, brighter than expectation is the ever returning *now* of Christmas. Why else, each time we greet in return, should happiness ring out in us like a peal of bells?

ELIZABETH BOWEN, *Anglo-Irish writer*

The one message of Christmas is the Christmas story. If it is false, we are doomed. If it is true, as it must be, it makes everything else in the world all right.

HARRY REASONER, *American television journalist*

The magic message of Christmas is that God gave us so much more than we can possibly give back!

NORMAN VINCENT PEALE, *American clergyman*

Christmas is but a big love affair to remove the wrinkles of the year with kindly remembrances.

JOHN WANAMAKER, *American merchant*

We consider Christmas as the encounter, the great encounter, the historical encounter, the decisive encounter, between God and mankind.

POPE PAUL VI

Christmas to an actor usually means an extra matinee.

EDDIE CANTOR, *American actor*

Of all the old festivals, that of Christmas awakens the strongest and most heartfelt associations. There is a tone of solemn and sacred feeling that blends with our conviviality, and lifts the spirit to a state of hallowed and elevated enjoyment.

WASHINGTON IRVING, *American writer*

I do hope your Christmas has had a little touch of Eternity in among the rush and pitter patter and all. It always seems such a mixing of this world and the next—but that after all *is* the idea!

EVELYN UNDERHILL, *English mystic*

To perceive Christmas through its wrapping becomes more difficult with every year.

E. B. WHITE, *American writer*

Just a hurried line . . . to tell a story which puts the contrast between *our* feast of the Nativity and all this ghastly "Xmas" racket at its lowest. My brother heard a woman on a bus say, as the bus passed a church with a Crib outside it, "Oh Lor'! They bring religion into everything. Look—they're dragging it even into Christmas now!"

C. S. LEWIS, *English writer*

There will probably always be voices raised to protest the commercialization of Christmas. But there is as much space in this vast land for those who want to keep it as a holy day as for those who want to rejoice in the holiday.

ROBERT OSTERMANN, *American writer*

Christmas is for children. But it is for grownups, too. Even if it is a headache, a chore, a nightmare, it is a period of necessary defrosting of chill and hidebound hearts.

LENORA MATTINGLY WEBER, *American writer*

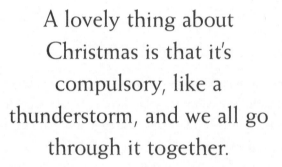

A lovely thing about Christmas is that it's compulsory, like a thunderstorm, and we all go through it together.

GARRISON KEILLOR,
American humorist

There are some people who want to throw their arms round you simply because it is Christmas; there are other people who want to strangle you simply because it is Christmas.

ROBERT LYND, *Anglo-Irish essayist and journalist*

It is my heart-warm and world-embracing Christmas hope and aspiration that all of us, the high, the low, the rich, the poor, the admired, the despised, the loved, the hated, the civilized, the savage (every man and brother of us all throughout the whole earth), may eventually be gathered together in a heaven of everlasting rest and peace and bliss, except the inventor of the telephone.

MARK TWAIN, *American writer*

Music awakens my Christmas spirit.

JULIE ANDREWS, *English actor*

Someone began to sing, "Come, all ye faithful!" I joined in and sang with the strangers all about me. I am not alone at all, I thought. I was never alone at all. And that, of course, is the message of Christmas. We are never alone. Not when the night is darkest, the wind coldest, the world seemingly most indifferent. For this is still the time God chooses.

TAYLOR CALDWELL, *American writer*

The Nativity brings us within touching distance, so to speak, of our spiritual birth in God through grace.

POPE JOHN PAUL II

The things we do at Christmas are touched with a certain extravagance, as beautiful, in some of its aspects, as the extravagance of Nature in June.

ROBERT COLLYER, *American clergyman*

Christmas . . . is not an external event at all, but a piece of one's home that one carries in one's heart: like a nursery story, its validity rests on exact repetition, so that it comes around every time as the evocation of one's whole life and particularly of the most distant bits of it in childhood.

FREYA STARK, *English travel writer and photographer*

The best part of Christmas is seeing it through the eyes of your children.

MICHELLE PFEIFFER, *American actor*

I'll be spending a typical American Christmas. My tree is from Canada, the ornaments from Hong Kong. The lights come from Japan—and the idea from Bethlehem.

ROBERT ORBEN, *American writer*

My idea of Christmas, whether old-fashioned or modern, is very simple: loving others.

BOB HOPE, *American comedian and actor*

If any of you have any quarrels, or misunderstandings, or coolnesses, or cold shoulders, or shynesses, or tiffs, or miffs, or huffs, with anyone else, just make friends before Christmas—you will be so much merrier if you do.

ELIZABETH GASKELL, *English novelist*

A perfectly managed Christmas correct in every detail is, like basted inside seams and letters answered by return, a sure sign of someone who hasn't enough to do.

KATHERINE WHITEHORN, *English journalist*

Let's not permit the crowds and the rush to crowd Christmas out of our hearts.

PETER MARSHALL, *American clergyman*

Christmas turns all wise souls from the surface that is time to the center that is eternity.

E. MERRILL ROOT, *American poet*

"Maybe Christmas," he thought,
"Doesn't come from a store.
"Maybe Christmas . . . perhaps . . . means a little bit more."

From How the Grinch Stole Christmas *by* DR. SEUSS

For me, the joy of Christmas is about knowing that I get my family members—my favorite people—to myself for long, lazy days, while the rest of the world doesn't care about work. It's about eating brunch and laughing at a movie and taking out all the old Christmas photos.

GOLDIE HAWN, *American actor*

Christmas is the glorious time of great Too-Much.

LEIGH HUNT, *English poet*

I never could see why people were so happy about Dickens's *A Christmas Carol* because I never had any confidence that Scrooge was going to be different the next day.

DR. KARL MENNINGER, *American psychiatrist*

I read Dickens's *Christmas Carol* to my family. What better reminder is there of the meaning of Christmas day?

ELEANOR ROOSEVELT, *American first lady*

Christmas is a bridge. We need bridges as the river of time flows past. Today's Christmas should mean creating happy homes for tomorrow and reliving those of yesterday.

GLADYS TABER, *American archaeologist*

Each of us creates our own special time at Christmas. We find our special ornaments, hang the mistletoe, and place the star as we have done before. There is a comforting certainty in the sameness—a promise of continuity.

LADY BIRD JOHNSON, *American first lady*

Christmas, too, is come. It is a visiting, unquiet, un-Quakerish season. I get more and more in love with solitude, and proportionately hampered with company.

CHARLES LAMB, *English essayist and critic*

How many observe Christ's birthday! How few, his precepts! 'Tis easier to keep holidays than commandments.

BENJAMIN FRANKLIN,
American statesman, scientist, and philosopher

Christmas makes the rest of the year worthwhile.

CHARLES SCHULZ, *American cartoonist*

The outdoor Christmas lights, green and red and gold and blue and twinkling, remind me that most people are that way all year round—kind, generous, friendly, and with an occasional moment of ecstasy. But Christmas is the only time they dare reveal themselves.

HARLAN MILLER, *American writer*

What a blessing Christmas is! What it does for friendship! Why, if there were no Christmas, we'd have to invent one, for it is the one season of the year when we can lay aside all gnawing worry, indulge in sentiment without censure, assume the carefree faith of childhood, and just plain "have fun."

D. D. MONROE

What I like about Christmas is that you can make people forget the past with the present.

DON MARQUIS, *American journalist and humorist*

I have always been subconsciously embarrassed by the "function" of Christmas and New Year's. The spirit of "loving kindness," that is presumed to come to a head like a boil once a year, when it has been magnificently concealed up to that moment!

JOHN BARRYMORE, *American actor*

And numerous indeed are the hearts to which Christmas brings a brief season of happiness and enjoyment. How many families, whose members have been dispersed and scattered far and wide, in the restless struggles of life, are then reunited, and meet once again in that happy state of companionship and mutual goodwill which is a source of such pure and unalloyed delight. . . .

CHARLES DICKENS, *English novelist*

So if a Christian is touched only once a year, the touching is still worth it, and maybe on some given Christmas, some quiet morning, the touch will take.

HARRY REASONER, *American television journalist*

Christmas, that time of the year when people descend into the bunker of the family.

BYRN ROBERTS

If Christmas didn't already exist, man would have had to invent it. There has to be at least one day in the year to remind us that we're here for something else besides our general cussedness.

ERIC SEVAREID, *American television journalist*

Christmas itself may be called into question;
If carried so far it creates indigestion.

RALPH BERGENGREN, *American author*

It is Christmas every time you let God love others through you. . . . Yes, it is Christmas every time you smile at your brother and offer him your hand.

MOTHER TERESA, *Albanian nun*

Whether they call it Yuletide, Noël, Weinachten, or Christmas, people around the earth thirst for its refreshment as the desert traveler for the oasis.

D. D. MONROE

Somehow not only for Christmas
But all the long year through,
The joy that you give to others
Is the joy that comes back to you.

JOHN GREENLEAF WHITTIER, *American poet*

Just for a few hours on Christmas Eve and Christmas Day, the stupid, harsh mechanism of the world runs down, and we permit ourselves to live according to untrammeled common sense, the unconquerable efficiency of good will.

CHRISTOPHER MORLEY, *American writer*

The world is large and complex, and sometimes there seems to be no sacred ground. But in tent and palace, in adobe hut and castle, in barrack prison and under lighted trees across the lands, the language of Christmas is universal.

MARCUS BACH, *American theologian*

Christmas is a box of tree ornaments that have become part of the family.

CHARLES SCHULZ, *American cartoonist*

Until one feels the spirit of Christmas—there is no Christmas. All else is outward display—so much tinsel and decorations. For it isn't the holly, it isn't the snow. It isn't the tree or the firelight's glow. It's the warmth that comes to the hearts of men when the Christmas spirit returns again.

Author Unknown

I wish we could put some
of the Christmas spirit in
jars and open a jar of
it every month.

HARLAN MILLER,
American writer

For most of us it can be a Happy Christmas if by happiness we mean that we have done with doubts, that we have set our hearts against fear, that we still believe in the Golden Rule for all mankind.

FRANKLIN DELANO ROOSEVELT,
32nd president of the United States

The secret of the best Christmases is everybody doing the same things all at the same time. You will all fall to and string cranberries and popcorn for the tree, and the bright lines each of you has a hold on will radiate from the tree like ribbons on a maypole. Everybody will have needles and thread in the mouth, you will all get in each other's way, but that is the art of doing Christmas right.

ROBERT P. TRISTRAM COFFIN, *American poet*

The best part of Christmas is sharing it with my daughter. I'm trying not to spoil her too much with gifts. I explain the meaning of the holiday and why it's important to be nice to others. I want her to see the true beauty of the world at this time of the year.

KIM BASINGER, *American actor*

Blessed by the Christmas sunshine, our natures, perhaps long leafless, bring forth new love, new kindness, new mercy, new compassion.

HELEN KELLER, *American writer and lecturer*

Remember
This December,
That love weighs more than gold!

JOSEPHINE DODGE BACON, *American writer*

There has been only one Christmas—the rest are anniversaries.

W. J. CAMERON

What was the first prophetic word that rang
When down the starry sky the angels sang,
That night they came as envoys of the Birth—
What word but peace, "peace and good will on earth?"

EDWIN MARKHAM, *American poet*

Blessed is the season that engages the whole world in a conspiracy of love!

HAMILTON WRIGHT MABIE, *American editor and critic*

Whatever else be lost among the years,
Let us keep Christmas still a shining thing.

GRACE NOLL CROWELL, *American poet*

How I wish we might be together these two Christmas days—I
should so love to see you in the studio again. I have been working hard lately, just because of that Christmas sentiment, and because feeling is not enough: one must express it in one's work.

VINCENT VAN GOGH, *Dutch painter*

It is impossible to conceive of any holiday that could take its
place, nor indeed would it seem that human wit could invent
another so adapted to humanity.

CHARLES DUDLEY WARNER, *American man of letters*

We hear the beating of wings over Bethlehem and a light that is not of the sun or of the stars shines in the midnight sky. Let the beauty of the story take away all narrowness, all thought of formal creeds. Let it be remembered as a story that has happened again and again, to men of many different races, that has been expressed through many religions, that has been called by many different names.

The New York Times, *December 25, 1937*

The antiquarians have disputed much and long about whether the event that Christmas commemorates can have taken place late in the month we call December. We have been told that this is the very height of the rainy season in Palestine, which it would be most unlikely to find either flocks or shepherds at night in the fields near Bethlehem. But it makes no difference to the solemn suggestiveness of the season, whether the exact date is right or wrong.

HERBERT LESLIE STEWART,
Canadian philosopher and professor

Christmas Past

All through November and December we watch it drawing nearer; we see the shop windows begin to glow with red and green and lively colors; we note the altered demeanor of bell-boys and janitors as the Date flows quietly toward us; we pass through the haggard perplexity of "Only Four Days More" when we suddenly realize it is too late to make our shopping list the display of lucid affectionate reasoning we had contemplated, and clutch wildly at grotesque tokens—and then (sweetest of all) comes the quiet calmness of Christmas Eve.

CHRISTOPHER MORLEY, *American writer*

On Christmas Eve, the faces of people are more alive than on any other day of the year.

CARL SANDBURG, *American poet*

Christmas Eve was a night of song that wrapped itself about you like a shawl. But it warmed more than your body. It warmed your heart . . . filled it, too, with melody that would last forever.

BESS STREETER ALDRICH, *American writer*

It is always so beautiful when the candles are lit to signify the new world, the new year, the new life. Our heavy little church is not unlike the cave where the birth of Jesus is so often pictured. The people knelt and prayed, shepherds and fishermen. I knelt too, and tried to turn my confused thoughts into some kind of charity and goodwill, to pray in my way.

From Possession *by* A. S. BYATT

This is the dear Christmas Eve, on which I have so often listened with impatience for your step, which was to usher us into the present-room. Today I have two children of my own to give presents to, who, they know not why, are full of happy wonder at the German Christmas-tree and its radiant candles.

PRINCE ALBERT,
husband of Queen Victoria, in a letter to his father

Then we each got a darning needle, a big one, and a ball of string. We strung the popcorn into long, long ropes, to hang upon the tree. But that was only half of it! There were stars to be cut out of kindergarten paper, red and green, and silver, and gold, and walnuts to be wrapped in gold paper, or painted with gold paint out of the paint-box that I had been given for my birthday. One got the paint into one's fingernails, and it smelled like bananas. And red apples to be polished, because a shiny apple makes a brave show on a tree. And when it was all finished, it was Christmas Eve.

DOROTHY THOMPSON, *American journalist*

There's a song in the air!
There's a star in the sky!
There's a mother's deep prayer
    And a Baby's low cry!
And the star rains its fire where the Beautiful sing,
For the manger of Bethlehem cradles a King.

JOSIAH GILBERT HOLLAND, *American editor*

The Yule-clog is a great log of wood, sometimes the root of a tree, brought into the house with great ceremony, on Christmas Eve, laid in the fireplace, and lighted with the brand of last year's clog. While it lasted there was great drinking, singing, and telling of tales. Sometimes it was accompanied by Christmas candles, but in the cottages the only light was from the ruddy blaze of the great wood fire.

The Yule-clog was to burn all night; if it went out, it was considered a sign of ill luck.

WASHINGTON IRVING, *American writer*

The day before Christmas, as we were walking along Canal Street, I stopped dead still, mesmerized by a magical object that I saw in the window of a big toy store. It was a model airplane large enough to sit in and pedal like a bicycle. It was green and had a red propeller.

I was convinced that if you pedaled fast enough it would take off and fly! . . . That night I prayed that Santa Claus would bring me the airplane.

TRUMAN CAPOTE, *American writer*

Christmas was the one occasion on which my mother surren-
dered to unabashed sentimentality. . . . She took girlish delight
in keeping her brightly wrapped gifts hidden in closets. Christmas Eve she spent in frenzies of baking—cakes, pies, ginger-
bread cookies cut and decorated to look like miniature brown
pine trees and Santa Clauses. In the afternoon she took Doris
and me to the street corner where trees were piled high and
searched through them until she found one that satisfied our
taste for fullness and symmetry.

        . . . She did not place her gifts under the tree that night
until Doris and I had gone to bed. We were far beyond believ-
ing in Santa Claus, but she insisted on preserving the forms of
the childhood myth that these were presents from some divine
philanthropist.

RUSSELL BAKER, *American writer*

Awake, glad heart! Get up, and sing!
It is the birthday of the King.

HENRY VAUGHAN, *English poet*

Christmas Eve afternoon we scrape together a nickel and go to the butcher's to buy Queenie's traditional gift, a good gnawable beef bone. The bone, wrapped in funny paper, is placed high in the tree near the silver star. Queenie knows it's there. She squats at the foot of the tree staring up in a trance of greed: when bedtime arrives she refuses to budge.

TRUMAN CAPOTE, *American writer*

A Christmas day, to be perfect, should be clear and cold, with holly branches in berry, a blazing fire, a dinner with mince pies, and games and forfeits in the evening. You cannot have it in perfection if you are very fine and fashionable. A Christmas evening should, if possible, finish with music. It carries off the excitement without abruptness, and sheds a repose over the conclusion of the enjoyment.

LEIGH HUNT, *English poet*

Christmas in Bethlehem. The ancient dream: a cold, clear night made brilliant by a glorious star, the smell of incense, shepherds and wise men falling to their knees in adoration of the sweet baby, the incarnation of perfect love.

LUCINDA FRANKS, *American writer*

They all were looking for a king
    To slay their foes and lift them high;
Thou cam'st, a little baby thing,
    That made a woman cry.

GEORGE MACDONALD, *British poet and novelist*

Heap on more wood!—the wind is chill;
But let it whistle as it will,
We'll keep our Christmas merry still.

SIR WALTER SCOTT, *Scottish poet, novelist, and historian*

I cannot let this day of grateful rejoicing pass without some communion with you. I am thankful for the many among the past that I have passed with you, and the remembrance of them fills me with pleasure.

ROBERT E. LEE, *American general,*
in a letter to his wife, December 25, 1861

christmas morning i
got up before the others and
ran
naked across the plank
floor into the front
room to see grandmama
sewing a new
button on my last year
ragdoll.

CAROL FREEMAN, *American poet*

Time was, with most of us, when
Christmas Day, encircling all our
limited world like a magic ring,
left nothing out for us to miss or
seek; bound together all our
home enjoyments, affections,
and hopes, grouped everything
and everyone around the
Christmas fire; and made the
little picture shining in our
bright young eyes, complete.

CHARLES DICKENS,
English novelist

It being a fine, light, moonshine morning, and so home round the city, and stopped and dropped money at five or six places, which I was the willinger to do, it being Christmas day, and so home, and there find my wife in bed, and Jane and the maids making pyes, and so I to bed, and slept well, and rose about nine, and to church.

SAMUEL PEPYS, *English diarist, December 25th, 1667*

There is nothing sadder in this world than to awake Christmas morning and not be a child. . . . Time, self-pity, apathy, bitterness, and exhaustion can take the Christmas out of the child, but you cannot take the child out of Christmas.

ERMA BOMBECK, *American humorist*

It is good to be children sometimes, and never better than at Christmas, when its mighty Founder was a child Himself.

CHARLES DICKENS, *English novelist*

When mother-love makes all things bright,

When joy comes with the morning light,

When children gather round their tree,

Thou Christmas Babe, we sing of thee.

TUDOR JENKS, *American humorist*

Thus my Christmas day was without dinner or presents, for the first time since I can remember. Yet it has been a very memorable day, and I feel as if I'd had a splendid feast seeing the poor babies wallow in turkey soup, and that every gift I put into their hands had come back to me in the dumb delight of their unchild-like faces trying to smile.

LOUISA MAY ALCOTT, *American writer*

Were I a philosopher, I should write a philosophy of toys, showing that nothing else in life need to be taken seriously, and that Christmas Day in the company of children is one of the few occasions on which men become entirely alive.

ROBERT LYND, *Anglo-Irish essayist and journalist*

I sometimes think we expect too much of Christmas Day. We try to crowd into it the long arrears of kindliness and humanity of the whole year. As for me, I like to take my Christmas a little at a time, all through the year. And thus I drift along into the holidays—let them overtake me unexpectedly—waking up some fine morning and suddenly saying to myself: "Why, this is Christmas Day!"

DAVID GRAYSON, *American journalist and author*

Christmas Day passed very quietly. The men had a holiday from work and the children from school and the churchgoers attended special Christmas services. Mothers who had young children would buy them an orange each and a handful of nuts; but, except at the end house and the inn, there was no hanging up of stockings, and those who had no kind elder sister or aunt in service to send them parcels got no Christmas presents.

FLORA THOMPSON, *English writer*

Mary the Mother
   Sang to her Son,
In a Bethlehem shed
   When the light was done.

"Jesus, Jesus,
   Little son, sleep;
The tall kings are gone,
   The lads with the sheep."

LIZETTE WOODWORTH REESE, *American poet*

If the lady of the household is ambitious, the bird is stuffed with oysters, and if she rules her husband, she orders him to purchase the oysters and turkey himself. Almost all the good old gentlemen consider it part of their religion to go down to Fulton Market, which is the aristocratic one.

The New York Times, *1874*

My sister sent a motorcar for us—so we were at Ripley in time for turkey and Christmas pudding. My God, what masses of food here, turkey, large tongues, a long wall of roast loin of pork, pork pies, sausages, mince pies, dark cakes covered with almonds, cheesecakes, lemon tarts, jellies, endless masses of food, with whisky, gin, port wine, burgundy, muscatel. It seems incredible. We played charades—the old people of 67 playing away harder than the young ones—and lit the Christmas tree, and drank healths, and sang and roared—Lord above. If only one hadn't all the while a sense the next week would be the same dreariness as before. What a good party we might have had, had we really felt free of the world.

D. H. LAWRENCE, *English writer*

Observe a little boy at a Christmas dinner, and his grandfather opposite him. What a world of secret similarity there is between them. How hope in one, and retrospection in the other, and appetite in both, meet over the same ground of plum pudding.

LEIGH HUNT, *English poet*

To secure a Christmas dinner was even more important than to procure a Christmas tree. If we chanced to be near a little town, no one rode through the place without throwing a calculating glance into every yard or about the door yard of the less pretentious huts. A chicken, a duck, or a turkey was quickly noted and the owner was called out to find a booted and spurred cavalryman at the door, who accosted him with the usual frontier salutation: "I say, stranger, can I engage my Christmas dinner of you?"

ELIZABETH BACON CUSTER, *widow of General George Custer*

How bless'd, how envied, were our life,
Could we but scape the poulterer's knife!
But man, curs'd man, on Turkeys preys,
And Christmas shorten all our days:
Sometimes with oysters we combine,
Sometimes assist the savory chine;
From the low peasant to the lord,
The Turkey smokes on every board.

JOHN GAY, *English poet*

We have a Christmas dinner next day because of the food voucher Mam got from the St. Vincent de Paul Society. We have sheep's head, cabbage, floury white potatoes, and a bottle of cider because it's Christmas.

From Angela's Ashes *by* FRANK MCCOURT

I shall manage to eat somewhere and get full—even if at a restaurant—but, God knows, I am still young enough to have a horror of Christmas by myself.

THOMAS WOLFE, *American novelist*

They had their Christmas dinner; they had their afternoon—safe and happy and uninterrupted. Five commonplace-looking folk in a commonplace-looking house, but the eye of love knew that this was not all. In the wide sea of their routine they had found and taken for their own this island day, unforgettable.

ZONA GALE, *American writer*

My younger sister and I looked in the fire, dreaming about a future we could not know and didn't want to talk about. After a long silence we succumbed to a little do-you-remember about the Christmases of our childhood. And soon we were laughing about how Father used to organize us for the shaking of the pecan trees, and how later round the hearth we cracked nuts for fruitcakes and chewy syrup candy, and the firecrackers and Roman candles we Southerners saved for Christmas, and the excitement and terror of hog killings on frosty dawns, and the sausages our grandmother made for the special Christmas breakfast, with just enough red pepper and sage.

LILLIAN SMITH, *American novelist and civil rights worker*

Whether it's Christmas or New Year's, I love the fact that everyone knows they can come to my house and be fed until they're stuffed. I cook the dinner my mother used to serve: turkey, stuffing, and pumpkin and chocolate pies.

JULIA ROBERTS, *American actor*

I don't remember ever eating an orange in the country except at Christmas. All the kids would get an orange apiece in their Christmas stockings and that was our citrus fruit for the year. The brisk fragrance released when the skin of an orange was torn— that seemed for me the flavor of Christmas, of a special time.

LEON HALE, *American journalist*

We watched all the Christmas movies, *Miracle on 34th Street* and *It's a Wonderful Life*, and when George Bailey's brother called him the richest man in town we sat there sobbing, and even my father cried silently. . . . We watched *A Christmas Carol*, the old black-and-white English version with Alastair Sim.

"There has quite literally never been a good film made of one of Dickens's novels, " my father said. . . . "It's not possible. The backbone of Dickens is physical description. It's the description that fails them."

From One True Thing *by* ANNA QUINDLEN

I'm dreaming of a white Christmas,
Just like the ones I used to know. . . .

IRVING BERLIN, *American composer and lyricist*

My love of Christmas has not diminished, and I am grateful to
have seen so many Christmases. But if I were asked which ones
stick in the memory most vividly, I would have to say those earliest ones.

JAMES BEARD, *American cook and cookbook writer*

From our earliest Christmas times, Santa Claus brought us toys
that instruct boys and girls (separately) how to build things—
stone blocks cut to the castle-building style, Tinker Toys, and
Erector sets.

EUDORA WELTY, *American novelist*

The song *White Christmas* is like an old Christmas memory: It inspires a happy sadness in the heart.

BING CROSBY, *American singer and actor*

As you get older, you may think Christmas has changed. It hasn't. It's you who have changed.

HARRY TRUMAN, *33rd president of the United States*

My fantasy for a perfect Christmas is set long ago in New England and includes a big family, church, dinner, and presents followed by singing and sledding.

GREGORY PECK, *American actor*

Sometimes I think our Christmas on the frontier was a greater event to us than to anyone in the states. We all had to do so much to make it a success.

ELIZABETH BACON CUSTER,
widow of General George Custer

Always on Christmas night there was music. An uncle played the fiddle, a cousin sang *Cherry Ripe* and another uncle sang *Drake's Drum*. It was very warm in the little house.

DYLAN THOMAS, *Welsh poet*

We stopped in a sliding slither, knocked loose our skis, and the three of us hiked up the hill toward the lights of the chalet. The lights looked very cheerful against the dark pines of the hill, and inside was a big Christmas tree and a real Christmas turkey dinner, the table shiny with silver, the glasses tall and thin stemmed, the bottles narrow-necked, the turkey large and brown and beautiful, the side dishes all present, and Ida serving in a new crisp apron. It was the kind of a Christmas you can only get on top of the world.

ERNEST HEMINGWAY, *American writer*

Christmas should be remembered for the smell of pine, oranges, ginger, and cloves.

EUGENE MCCARTHY, *American politician*

On Christmas morning the children awoke early and came in to see their toys. They were followed by the Negro women, who one after another "caught" us by wishing us a merry Christmas before we could say it to them, which gave them a right to a gift. Of course, there was a present for every one, small though it might be, and one who had been born and brought up at our plantation was vocal in her admiration of a gay handkerchief.

The wife of Confederate President Jefferson Davis,
recalling the Christmas of 1864 in the midst of the Civil War

When I was a kid we didn't have much money, so the holidays were never about presents. They were about that peaceful feeling you got when everyday things were made more beautiful. I enjoyed watching the *Nutcracker* on television and dreaming I could be one of the girls in those beautiful dresses.

SARAH JESSICA PARKER, *American actor*

The best Christmas was the one when I was five, before worldliness and wisdom began to set in.

CHARLES KURALT, *American television correspondent*

Momma was so happy that Christmas, all the food folks brought us and Mister Bob giving us more credit, and Momma even talked the electric man into turning the lights on again. . . .

DICK GREGORY, *American humorist*

It was a strange kind of Christmas, but, perhaps, in that Narayangunj bazaar we were in a way closer to Bethlehem than in the bells and revelry, the eating and drinking and tinsel of England. The humble dim lit interior of the huts we passed might have been the stable cave; a sari might have been the line of Mary's veil. . . . The oil lamp on the floor was the same shape as the lamps they had in Bethlehem; a carpenter, working late by its light, his brown arms glistening as he planed a piece of wood, might have been Joseph, and there was always an ox kneeling and ruminating in the shadows. . . . We, of course, saw or thought none of this: it was all too familiar and we were too tired, tired with an intoxication of satisfaction and happiness.

JON AND RUMER GODDEN, *English novelists*

The wintry blast goes wailing by,
The snow is falling overhead;
I hear the lonely sentry's tread,
And distant watch-fires light the sky.

Dim forms go flitting through the gloom;
The soldiers cluster round the blaze
To talk of other Christmas days,
And softly speak of home and home.

WILLIAM G. MCCABE,
serving in the Army of West Virginia, 1862

There were not many white Christmases in our part of Wales in my childhood—perhaps only one or two—but Christmas cards and Dickens and Dylan Thomas and wishful memory have turned them all into white.

RICHARD BURTON, *Welsh actor*

Twenty-five years ago, Christmas was not the burden that it is now; There was less haggling and weighing, less *quid pro quo*, less fatigue of body, less weariness of soul; and, most of all, there was less loading up with trash.

MARGARET DELAND, *American writer*

In the old days, it was not called the Holiday Season: the Christians called it Christmas and went to church; the Jews called it Chanukah and went to synagogue; the atheists went to parties and drank. People passing each other on the street would say "Merry Christmas!" or "Happy Chanukah!" or (to the atheists) "Look out for the wall!"

DAVE BARRY, *American humorist*

When Imogene had asked me what the pageant was about, I told her it was about Jesus, but that was just part of it. It was about a new baby, and his mother and father who were in a lot of trouble—no money, no place to go, no doctor, nobody they knew. And then, arriving from the East (like my uncle from New Jersey) some rich friends.

BARBARA ROBINSON, *American writer*

At the peep of day we were aroused by the voice of my good grandfather, who planted himself in the stairway and shouted in a stentorian tone, "I wish you all a Merry Christmas!" The contest was as to who should give the salutation first, and the old gentleman determined to get the start of us by sounding his greeting to the family before we were out of our rooms. Then came a race for the chimney corner; all the stockings came down quicker than they had gone up.

THEODORE LEDYARD CUYLER, *American clergyman*

Happy, happy Christmas, that can win us back to the delusions of our childish days; that can recall to the old man the pleasures of his youth; that can transport the sailor and the traveler, thousands of miles away, back to his own fireside and his quiet home!

CHARLES DICKENS, *English novelist*

We speak of a Merry Christmas,
And many a Happy New Year;
But each in his heart is thinking
Of those that are not here.

HENRY WADSWORTH LONGFELLOW, *American poet*

It must be allowed that the regular recurrence of annual festivals among the same individuals has, as life advances, something in it that is melancholy. We meet on such occasions like the survivors of some perilous expedition, wounded and weakened ourselves, and looking through the diminished ranks of those who remain, while we think of those who are no more.

SIR WALTER SCOTT, *Scottish novelist, poet, and historian*

How many old recollections, and how many dormant sympathies, does Christmas time awaken!

CHARLES DICKENS, *English novelist*

There are few sensations more painful, than, in the midst of deep grief, to know that the season that we have always associated with mirth and rejoicing is at hand.

SARAH J. HALE, *American writer*

Sitting here, I incontinently find myself holding a levee of departed Christmas nights. Silently, and without special call, into my study of imagination come these apparitions, clad in snowy mantles, brooched and gemmed with frosts. Their numbers I do not care to count, for I know they are the numbers of many years. The visages of two or three are sad enough, but on the whole 'tis a congregation of jolly ghosts. The nostrils of my memory are assailed by a faint odor of plum pudding and burnt brandy. I hear a sound as of light music, a whisk of women's dresses whirled round in dance, a click as of glasses pledged by friends.

ALEXANDER SMITH, *Scottish poet, writer, and novelist*

Bah Humbug!

Every year, in the deep midwinter, there descends upon this world a terrible fortnight. . . . Every shop is a choked mass of humanity . . . nerves are jangled and frayed, purses emptied to no purpose, all amusements and all occupations suspended in favor of frightful businesses with brown paper, string, letters, cards, stamps, and crammed post offices. This period is doubtless a foretaste of whatever purgatory lies in store for human creatures.

ROSE MACAULAY, *English writer*

I feel exactly as you do about the horrid commercial racket they have made out of Christmas. I send no cards and give no presents except to children.

C. S. LEWIS, *English writer*

We'll bet that folks who spell Christmas "Xmas" leave their greeting cards unsealed so they'll go cheaper.

KIN HUBBARD, *American humorist*

Sending Christmas cards too early is not only ineffective but can be humiliating for the sender. It reveals one's position, discloses the size and quality of card, exposing oneself to the possibility of a devastating counter-attack. On the other hand, a very late Christmas card runs the risk of negating the recipient's ability to respond, and reduces one's total card count.

WILLIAM CONNOR, *English writer*

How utterly ridiculous you'd feel,
How damned unpleasant,
If you sent just a card to us
And *we* sent *you* a present.

RING LARDNER, *American humorist and short-story writer*

What do people mean by sending you a dozen Christmas cards during the festive season, and not deigning to send you three lines by way of a letter during the rest of the year?

J. ASHBY-STERRY, *English poet*

The Christmas season has come to mean the period when the public plays Santa Claus to the merchants.

JOHN ANDREW HOLMES

Christmas will soon be at our throats.

P. G. WODEHOUSE, *English humorous novelist*

In the United States Christmas has become the rape of an idea.

RICHARD BACH, *American writer*

There is a remarkable breakdown of taste and intelligence at Christmastime. Mature responsible men wear neckties made out of holly leaves and drink alcoholic beverages with raw eggs and cottage cheese in them.

P. J. O'ROURKE, *American humorist*

Something in me resists the calendar expectation of happiness. Merry Christmas yourself! It mutters as it shapes a ghostly grin.

J. B. PRIESTLEY, *English writer*

Let us . . . make a compact that, if we are both alive next year, whenever we write to one another it shall *not* be at Christmas time. That period is becoming a sort of nightmare to me—it means endless quill-driving!

C. S. LEWIS, *English writer*

Christmas in Australia is a gigantic mistake.

MARCUS CLARKE, *Australian writer*

I hate, loathe, and despise Christmas. It's a time when single people have to take cover or get out of town.

KRISTIN HUNTER, *American writer*

Early in life I developed a distaste for the Cratchits that time has not sweetened. I do not think I was an embittered child, but the Cratchits' aggressive worthiness, their bravely borne poverty, their exultation over that wretched goose, disgusted me. I particularly disliked Tiny Tim (a part always played by a girl because girls had superior powers of looking moribund and worthy at the same time) and when he chirped, "God bless us every one!" my mental response was akin to Sam Goldwyn's famous phrase, "Include me out!"

ROBERTSON DAVIES, *Canadian writer*

I find it difficult to believe in Father Christmas. If he is the jolly old gentleman he is always said to be, why doesn't he behave as such? How is it that the presents go so often to the wrong people?

A. A. MILNE, *English author*

Evidently Christmas was an unmitigated joy only for the people who inhabited department-store brochures and seasonal television specials. For everyone else the day seemed to be a trip across a minefield seeded with resurrected family feuds, exacerbated loneliness, emotional excess, and the inevitable disappointments that arise when expectations fall far short of reality.

JOYCE REBETA-BURDITT,
American programming executive and novelist

The prospect of Christmas appalls me.

EVELYN WAUGH, *English novelist, satirist, and biographer*

Christmas is a time when kids tell Santa what they want and adults pay for it.

RICHARD LAMM, *American political leader*

1. Try to avoid giving (and receiving) extremely expensive gifts, particularly the heavily advertised fad/status symbol items that are often not very useful or practical.
2. Make every effort to use cash rather then credit cards to pay for the items that you do purchase.
3. Emphasize gifts that involve thought and originality, such as handicraft items that you make yourself.
4. Celebrate and enjoy the holidays but remember that a Merry Christmas is not for sale in any store for any amount of money.

The Four Principles of the Society to Curtail Ridiculous,
Outrageous, and Ostentatious Gift Exchanges (SCROOGE),
an American group founded in 1979

Christmas Wrap-Up

When all the tinsel has been laid away,
   The tree is stripped, the fevered rush is past—
You still have trees, a hill, a child at play,
   And love, and prayer, and fadeless things that last.

                        ANNA BLAKE MEZQUIDA

Christmas has come and gone, and I—to speak selfishly—am glad of it. The season always gives me the blues in spite of myself, though I manage to get a good deal of pleasure from thinking of the multitudes of happy kids in various parts of the world.

                  EDWIN ARLINGTON ROBINSON, *American poet*

Christmas is over and Business is Business.

FRANKLIN PIERCE ADAMS, *American journalist*

Christmas is the feast of the beginnings, of instinctive happy childhood. . . . It blends with the thought of the New Year, with its hope and promise, laid in the cradle of Time.

CLEMENT A. MILES, *writer*

Down with the rosemary and so
Down with the bay and mistletoe,
Down with the holly, ivy, all
Wherewith ye deck'd the Christmas hall;
That so the superstitious find
No one least branch there left behind:
For look! How many leaves there be
Neglect there, Maids, trust to me,
So many goblins you shall see.

ROBERT HERRICK, *English poet and clergyman*

The days between Christmas Day and New Year's were allowed the slaves as holidays. During these days all regular work was suspended, and there was nothing to do but keep fires and look after the stock. We regarded this time as our own by the grace of our masters, and we therefore used it or abused it as we pleased. Those who had families at a distance were expected to visit them and spend with them the entire week. The young slaves or the unmarried ones were expected to see to the animals and attend to incidental duties at home. . . . But the majority spent the holidays in sports, ball playing, wrestling, boxing, running, footraces, dancing, and drinking whiskey; and this latter mode was generally most agreeable to their masters. A slave who would work during the holidays was thought by his master undeserving of holidays.

FREDERICK DOUGLASS, *American writer*

Love and joy come to you
And a joyful Christmas, too;
And God bless you and send
You a Happy New Year.

Author Unknown

New Year's Eve was our family ritual, our Christmas morning, our Fourth of July. It was the night on which we gathered, no matter where else we might have been tempted to go, to discover anew both how safe and how costly it was to be together. It was the night on which we brooded and smiled, ate too much and drank too little, and waltzed with each other at midnight. It was also the night that was never the way I hoped it would turn out to be.

From New Year's Eve *by* LISA GRUNWALD

New Year's Eve is like every other night; there is no pause in the march of the universe, no breathless moment of silence among created things that the passage of another twelve months may be noted; and yet no man has quite the same thoughts this evening that come with the coming of darkness on other nights.

HAMILTON WRIGHT MABIE, *American editor and critic*

No one ever regarded the first of January with indifference. It is the nativity of our common Adam.

CHARLES LAMB, *English essayist and critic*

Get up, good wife, and shake your feathers,
And dinna think that we are beggars;
For we are bairns come out to play,
Get up and gie'us our Hogmanay.

Traditional Scottish New Year's song

Ring out the old, ring in the new,
    Ring, happy bells, across the snow;
    The year is going, let him go;
Ring out the false, ring in the true.

ALFRED, LORD TENNYSON, *English poet*

And now let us believe in a long year that is given to us, new,
untouched, full of things that have never been, full of work that
has never been done, full of tasks, claims, and demands; and let
us see that we learn to take it without letting fall too much of
what it has to bestow upon those who demand of it necessary,
serious, and great things.

RAINER MARIA RILKE, *German poet*

A year has passed—another has commenced. These solemn divisions of time influence our feelings as they recur. Yet there is nothing in it, for every day in the year closes a twelvemonth as well as the 31st of December.

SIR WALTER SCOTT, *Scottish poet and novelist*

Thus times do shift—each thing his turn does hold;
New things succeed, as former things grow old.

ROBERT HERRICK, *English poet and clergyman*

Drop the last year into the perfect limbo of the past. Let it go, for it was imperfect, and thank God that it can go.

BROOKS ATKINSON, *American drama critic and essayist*

On the approach of a New Year, we, too, can believe in something better than experience has justified us in hoping for.

ROBERT LYND, *Anglo-Irish essayist and journalist*

Year's end is neither an end
nor a beginning, but a going
on, with all the wisdom that
experience can instill in us.

HAL BORLAND,
American newspaperman